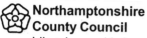

**Northamptonshire
County Council**
Libraries and Information Service

~~07 NOV 2005~~ Cwn

25/03/08 Cwn

Northamptonshire
DISCARDED
Libraries

OS ✓

ROUTH, K.

Down's syndrome

Please return or renew this item by the last date shown.
You may renew items (unless they have been requested
by another customer) by telephoning, writing to or calling
in at any library.   100% recycled paper   *BKS 1 (5/95)*

Sch

Need to Know

Down's Syndrome

Kristina Routh

www.heinemann.co.uk/library

Visit our website to find out more information about **Heinemann Library** books.

To order:

 Phone 44 (0) 1865 888066

 Send a fax to 44 (0) 1865 314091

Visit the Heinemann Bookshop at www.heinemann.co.uk/library to browse our catalogue and order online.

Produced by Monkey Puzzle Media Ltd
Gissing's Farm, Fressingfield, Suffolk IP21 5SH, UK

First published in Great Britain by Heinemann Library, Halley Court, Jordan Hill, Oxford OX2 8EJ, part of Harcourt Education.
Heinemann is a registered trademark of Harcourt Education Ltd.

Editorial: Katie Orchard
Design: Jamie Asher
Picture Research: Sally Cole
Consultant: Susannah Seyman, Down's Syndrome
  Association, UK
Production: Viv Hitchens

Originated by Ambassador Litho Ltd
Printed and bound in Hong Kong, China by
  South China Printing Company

ISBN 0 431 18843 2
08 07 06 05 04
10 9 8 7 6 5 4 3 2 1

Some names in this text have been changed to protect the privacy of the individuals quoted.

British Library Cataloguing in Publication Data
Routh, Kristina
  Down's syndrome. – (Need to know)
  1.Down's syndrome - Juvenile literature
  I.Title
  616.8'58842

Acknowledgements
The publishers would like to thank the following for permission to reproduce photographs: AKG-images p. 9 (Erich Lessing); Corbis p. 27 (Ricki Rosen/Saba); Down's Syndrome Association pp. 1, 5, 17, 18 (Sarah Hannant), 19 (Stephen Leighton), 23, 25, 41, 47, 50 (Stephen Leighton); John Birdsall Photography pp. 32, 38, 39, 51; Mary Evans Picture Library p. 10; Photofusion pp. 14 (M. Hawkins), 31 (Brian Mitchell), 33 (Paula Sollaway); Rex Features p. 45 (Schwartz/Sipa); Riding for the Disabled Association (incorporating Carriage Driving) p. 46; Science Photo Library pp. 12 (Robin Laurance), 13 (James King-Holmes/ICRF), 15 (Dr. Yorgos Nikas), 16 (Mauro Fermariello), 21 (Hattie Young), 35 (Hattie Young), 37 (Mauro Fermariello), 43 (BSIP Laurent), 49 (Ed Young); Topham Picturepoint/Image Works pp. 4 (Peter Hvizdar), 7 (Michael Greenlar), 29 (Ellen Senisi), 30 (Michael Greenlar); Wellcome Trust Photo Library p. 11.

Cover photographs reproduced with permission of SPL (Lauren Shear) and SPL (L. Willatt, East Anglian Regional Genetics Service).

Every effort has been made to contact copyright holders of any material reproduced in this book. Any omissions will be rectified in subsequent printings if notice is given to the publishers.

The publishers would like to thank the Down's Syndrome Association and the Riding for the Disabled Association for their help in providing photographs for this title.

Contents

Any words appearing in the text in bold, **like this**,
are explained in the Glossary.

Down's syndrome

There are people with Down's syndrome in every society in the world. Named after John Langdon Down, the man who first described it, Down's syndrome is a genetic condition. It is caused by the presence of an extra **chromosome**, a structure that carries the genetic information in each cell. A baby with Down's syndrome will always have it; the condition is part of who they are.

Probably the first thing anyone notices is that people with Down's syndrome tend to share some physical features. But this is only a passing similarity because people with Down's syndrome are all individuals who look like their parents, brothers and sisters, just like everyone else.

People with Down's syndrome all have a learning disability. This means that on average young children are slower to reach the childhood **milestones** such as crawling, walking and talking. Older children with Down's syndrome may take longer to learn to read and write, and may need specially adapted lessons in school. Young people and adults with Down's syndrome may take longer to learn how to care for themselves independently and may find it harder to find suitable jobs. In some people this learning disability is very severe and they may need special care all their lives.

Special Olympian Mary Beth Delaney (left) practises for a show with Olympic gold medalist Kristi Yamaguchi at the International Skating Center, Connecticut, USA.

4

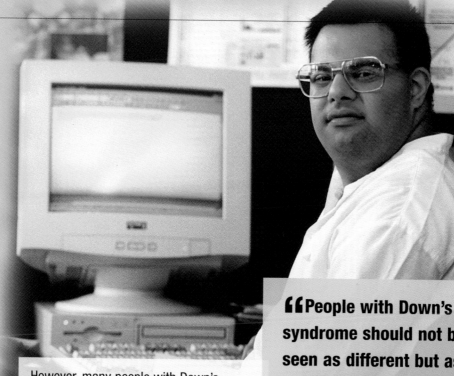

However, many people with Down's syndrome manage well in **mainstream schools**, pass public examinations, drive, play musical instruments, succeed at sports and even act on television. And many have found useful and enjoyable jobs and set up their own homes.

Health issues

In the past, people with the condition often died soon after birth. However, with modern healthcare this is now unusual. Although people with Down's syndrome may not, on average, live for as long as people who do not have the condition, many can now look forward to a life of over 60 years.

❝People with Down's syndrome should not be seen as different but as people who happen to have some additional needs.❞

(Sue Buckley, The Down's Syndrome Educational Trust, UK)

Down's syndrome or Down syndrome?

Different countries use different names for Down's syndrome. Down's syndrome is the term used in the UK, and the one that is used throughout this book. In some other countries, such as Australia and the USA, this condition is usually referred to as Down syndrome.

What is Down's syndrome?

Down's syndrome is a genetic condition. This means that it is present from the time a baby is **conceived**. It is not a disease that a baby catches, like a cold or the 'flu. And it is not caused by difficulties whilst a baby is growing in the womb.

Genetics

People with Down's syndrome have an extra piece of genetic material – three copies of **chromosome** 21 instead of the usual two (this is explained in full on pages 12–13). Having too much genetic information can affect the way a baby grows and develops, leading to a wide variety of different health issues. Not everyone with Down's syndrome will have the same problems, and some will be less affected than others.

Some people with Down's syndrome never have any specific health issues. However, some medical conditions are more common in people with Down's syndrome than in the general population.

These include abnormalities of the heart, difficulties with vision and hearing, thyroid problems, and infections of the **respiratory tract** (see pages 36–41). With good medical care most of these conditions can be picked up early and treated successfully.

Learning difficulties

People with Down's syndrome all have a certain degree of learning disability. This means that they are slower to learn new things than other people may be. But the ability to learn can vary enormously from one person to another.

“Remember that I am a person first and above all. The Down's syndrome is a part of me, but it is not my full identity.”

(Kay, USA, aged 40, who has Down's syndrome)

Kay's story

Kay is 40 and she has Down's syndrome. She lives with her parents in Texas, USA. Remembering her school days, Kay says, 'I was slow in learning but had wonderful first- and second-grade teachers that helped me. I had my struggles in school but I graduated from high school in 1980. I was 19.'

Kay has done many jobs in her life but is not employed at the moment due to poor health. Still, she keeps busy. Kay explains, 'I volunteer in my community, I help in the library.'

Many people are surprised that Kay can read and write so well. 'I love to read and even write my own poetry. Believe it or not, we don't all fit the stereotype idea that some people still have of us all!' says Kay.

With support from teachers and family, many children with Down's syndrome begin to enjoy reading and writing.

History of Down's syndrome

Down's syndrome has probably been present throughout the whole of human history. Archaeologists in Germany have found a skull of a young child dating back to 350 BC, which showed the characteristics of Down's syndrome. Another, similar skull from around the 10th century was found in Leicestershire, in the UK. However, there is little mention of Down's syndrome in ancient writings. This may well be because until recent years, due to poor healthcare, most of the babies born with Down's syndrome died soon after birth or in early childhood.

Life in early societies

Before the beginning of industrialization, most people made a living by working on the land and raising animals. There was no reason for the majority of people to learn how to read and write, or perform complex tasks. In this kind of community, which still exists in many developing countries today, a person with a learning disability such as Down's syndrome could often cope quite well. But, during the last three or four hundred years, as the population increased and people moved into towns and cities, life became more complicated. Without a lot of family support, people with Down's syndrome would have found it much harder to cope in these situations.

Differing ideas

Throughout history different societies have treated people with Down's syndrome in different ways. People are often scared of anyone who is different, either physically or mentally. In some societies, such as in ancient Greece, the birth of such a baby was seen as a punishment inflicted on the parents by the gods. Early Roman law even allowed a father to kill a child born with any deformities. Along with other babies with physical and mental disabilities, babies with Down's syndrome in these societies were thought to be of little value.

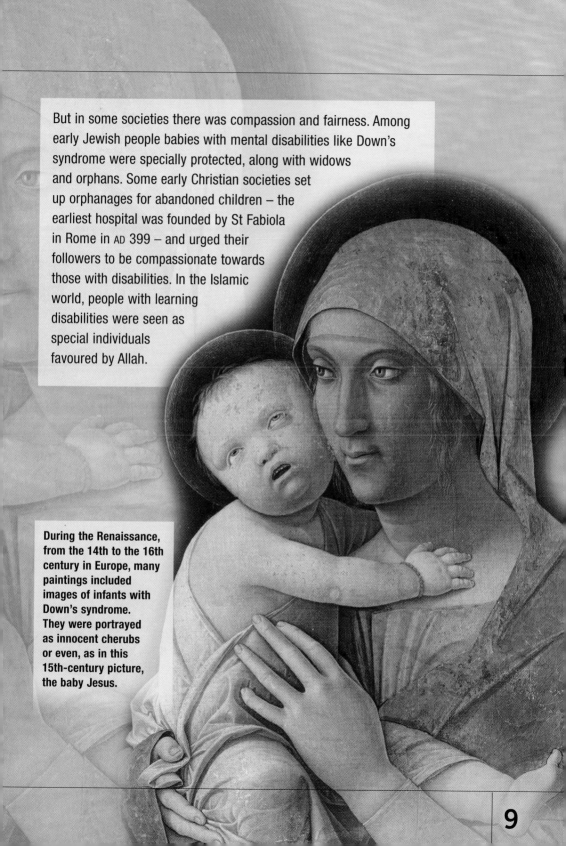

But in some societies there was compassion and fairness. Among early Jewish people babies with mental disabilities like Down's syndrome were specially protected, along with widows and orphans. Some early Christian societies set up orphanages for abandoned children – the earliest hospital was founded by St Fabiola in Rome in AD 399 – and urged their followers to be compassionate towards those with disabilities. In the Islamic world, people with learning disabilities were seen as special individuals favoured by Allah.

During the Renaissance, from the 14th to the 16th century in Europe, many paintings included images of infants with Down's syndrome. They were portrayed as innocent cherubs or even, as in this 15th-century picture, the baby Jesus.

Into modern times

For hundreds of years, life has been hard for those with Down's syndrome. While most died in infancy, the rest were frequently abandoned by their families. Between 1690 and 1720, each year about a thousand children were abandoned in England alone. They were often placed in institutions for the insane.

Down's syndrome is named after John Langdon Down, a doctor who worked in England in the mid-19th century. He saw many children with learning disabilities and noticed that many shared similar characteristics. He first described these in 1866. It was not until 1959 that Professor Jerome Lejeune of France discovered that Down's syndrome was due to the presence of an extra **chromosome** (see page 12).

During the 17th and 18th centuries, many people with Down's syndrome were sent to institutions for the insane, such as the famous Bedlam Hospital in London (pictured below).

The 20th century

During the 20th century, many people with disabilities were killed by the Nazis before and during the Second World War (1939–1945). Even well-meaning people believed that babies born with Down's syndrome would be better off in institutions. Parents were often told to forget about their child with Down's syndrome, as though he or she had died. Even if the child stayed within the family they were unlikely to receive any education.

It was not until the 1970s that, in countries such as the UK, children with Down's syndrome became entitled to education by law. Special schools were set up for those with learning disabilities. Over the last 30 years, great progress has been made in raising public awareness of this condition. Most babies with Down's syndrome now stay with their families, children now have the right to be taught in **mainstream schools**, and improved healthcare has vastly increased their **life expectancy** (see page 19).

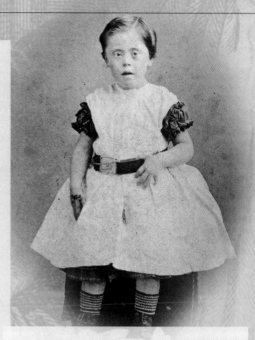

In the past many children with Down's syndrome died at birth or were put in institutions. This young Edwardian girl seems to have been luckier.

Mongolism – an unacceptable name

John Langdon Down thought that children with Down's syndrome looked like people from Mongolia, in Asia. For the next hundred years people with Down's syndrome were referred to as 'Mongols' or 'suffering from **Mongolism**'. This term is now considered very unkind. It is inaccurate and gives the impression that the only important thing about a person with Down's syndrome is their medical condition. People with Down's syndrome have the right to be referred to in a way which makes it clear that they are people first, and that their condition is just one part of who they are.

What causes Down's syndrome?

Down's syndrome is caused by the presence of an extra **chromosome** in the body's cells. Chromosomes are tiny, threadlike structures within each cell in the body that carry genetic information – all the instructions for building and running the body. This information is in the form of a code, which determines all the characteristics that have been passed down to a person from their parents.

Each cell should contain 46 paired chromosomes – half come from each parent when the sperm and the egg join together at conception. Scientists have given the chromosomes numbers so that they know which ones they are referring to when they talk about them. There are two each of chromosome 1, chromosome 2, chromosome 3 and so on, all the way up to 22. That makes 44. The last two are called the 'sex chromosomes' (which determine whether a baby is male or female) and are known as X and Y.

Scientists study chromosomes to find out more about genetic diseases such as Down's syndrome.

Extra chromosomes

Someone with Down's syndrome has an extra copy of chromosome 21 – so there are three instead of two. Down's syndrome is sometimes called '**trisomy 21**' ('tri' means three and 'somy' comes from the word 'chromosome'). Chromosome 21 is one of the smallest and is thought to carry around 1 per cent of all the body's genes. The extra copy of these genes causes problems in the development of a growing baby. At the moment, no one knows exactly how this happens, although a lot of research is being carried out.

This process can happen with other chromosomes. Occasionally babies are born who have an extra chromosome 13 or 18. These chromosomes are both much bigger than chromosome 21 and so contain a lot more genetic material. This causes more problems for the baby, who will usually be born quite severely disabled. Sometimes there is an extra X or Y chromosome. This does not seem to cause too much harm. But if one of the other chromosomes is involved, the **foetus** (the unborn child) is so abnormal that it does not usually survive long enough to be born, and the mother has a **miscarriage.**

Different types of Down's syndrome

There are three types of Down's syndrome: standard **trisomy** 21, **translocation** and **mosaicism**. The difference between these types of Down's syndrome is quite complicated, but the outcome is much the same in each case. The only way to tell the difference between these types is by studying a blood sample of an individual with Down's syndrome to look at the **chromosomes**.

When a woman becomes pregnant there is no way of preventing the unborn baby from being affected by Down's syndrome.

Standard trisomy 21

Standard trisomy 21 is by far the most common kind of Down's syndrome, accounting for around 95 per cent of all cases. Someone with standard trisomy 21 has an extra copy of chromosome 21 in each of their cells. This extra copy came from either the mother's egg or from the father's sperm. It makes no difference to the baby whether the extra chromosome came from the mother or father. No one knows why this happens and there is no known way of preventing it. It is known that older women are more likely to have a baby with this type of Down's syndrome but, again, it is not clear why.

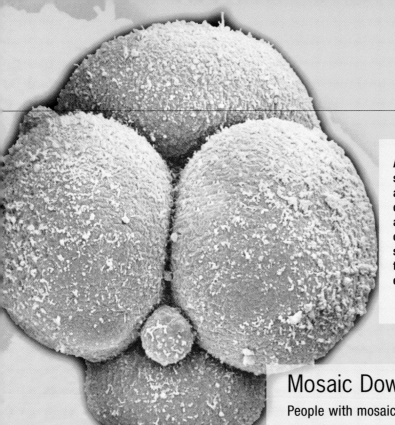

A baby grows from a single cell that divides and grows over and over again, until there are many millions of cells. In mosaic Down's syndrome, some of these cells contain an extra chromosome 21.

Mosaic Down's syndrome

People with mosaic Down's syndrome, around 2 per cent of cases, have an extra chromosome 21 in only some of their cells. When the sperm fertilizes the egg the cell that is formed has to divide repeatedly and grow to form the many new cells that make up the baby. In mosaic Down's syndrome there is a mistake during these divisions. This leads to an extra chromosome 21 in only some cells, other cells are unaffected.

In mosaic Down's syndrome the proportion of cells in the body which have the extra chromosome 21 can vary greatly. Depending on how many cells are abnormal, and where in the body those cells exist, the individual with mosaic Down's syndrome may have fewer of the features of Down's syndrome than those with the other types.

Translocation

In about 3 per cent of cases of Down's syndrome there are the normal two chromosome 21's plus an extra piece of chromosome 21, which is stuck to another chromosome (usually 14). This extra piece of chromosome 21 has been broken off from its original position and moved to the new chromosome by a process known as translocation – which just means 'moving across'. This type of Down's syndrome can very occasionally be inherited (passed from one generation to the next).

Characteristics of Down's syndrome

It is natural for parents who have a baby with Down's syndrome to wonder what their child will look like when they get older. People with Down's syndrome look like their parents, brothers and sisters just as much as everyone else does. However, there are some common characteristics that tend to be shared by those with Down's syndrome (see box on page 17).

Examining a new baby

When a baby is born it is always carefully checked over by medical staff. One of the things being looked for are physical signs of genetic conditions such as Down's syndrome. If several of these features are present in the baby then Down's syndrome will be suspected and blood tests will be performed to confirm it. Sometimes, however, the characteristic signs of Down's syndrome are not so obvious and no one suspects the diagnosis for weeks or even months. Not every person with Down's syndrome will have all of the physical features associated with the condition. Some people who do not have Down's syndrome may also have one or two of these features.

Common features of Down's syndrome

Some of the common physical features associated with Down's syndrome are listed below:

• Looser muscles and joints, which make the baby seem 'floppy'. The correct medical term for this is **hypotonia**.

• A rather flat face with a flattened bridge of the nose.

• Eyes that tend to slant upwards and outwards. There are often folds of skin between the lids in the corner of the eyes. The correct medical term for these is **'epicanthic' folds**.

• A small mouth, which seems to make the tongue look a bit too big. Looseness in the muscles sometimes makes the tongue stick out.

• Broad hands with short fingers. The little finger may curl in a bit and there may be only a single crease across the palm.

• The feet may show a deep space between the first and second toe. This crease is known as a 'sandal gap'.

• A lower than average birth-weight and length. Adults with Down's syndrome are, on average, shorter than others.

❝Twelve hours after Ellie was born the doctor asked us what we knew about Down syndrome. Our world turned upside down.❞

(Jenny, USA, mother of Ellie, now 22, who has Down's syndrome. Source: National Association for Down Syndrome, USA)

Who is affected?

There are many people with Down's syndrome living all over the world. Every year many babies are born with the condition. It is the most common cause of a learning disability, and the most common chromosomal abnormality.

For every 800 to 1000 babies that are born, one will have Down's syndrome.

A large country like the USA, for instance, has as many as 350,000 people with Down's syndrome. It is not known why, but boys seem slightly more likely to have it than girls. Not all countries keep accurate records of the numbers of babies born with Down's syndrome or other medical conditions, but many do. For example in the USA about 4000 babies are born each year with Down's syndrome, in the UK about 700 and in Australia 400.

Miscarriages

A **miscarriage** is when a pregnancy ends before the baby has chance to develop and be born. This usually happens at a very early stage of a pregnancy. Miscarriages are very common and there are many different causes. One cause is when the **foetus** has an abnormality in the **chromosomes**, such as Down's syndrome. One scientific study showed that only 25 per cent of all foetuses with Down's syndrome survive to be born. So for every baby that is born with Down's syndrome there are at least three more foetuses that are lost in miscarriages.

Life expectancy

People with Down's syndrome today are living healthier and longer lives than ever before. About 80 years ago it was expected that most children with Down's syndrome would die before the age of six. Even 40 years ago as many as three out of five children with Down's syndrome died before their fifth birthday and few reached adulthood. Many died because of the various **heart defects** that are common in Down's syndrome (see page 36).

Since then there have been great improvements in medical care, both for pregnant women, and for babies and children with medical problems. Today, in developed countries such as the USA, UK and Australia, the average **life expectancy** is around 75–80 years. For people with Down's syndrome living in those countries, the life expectancy is around 55 years. But some may live into their 80s.

People with Down's syndrome are now living longer then ever before.

Can Down's syndrome be prevented?

Every day throughout the world mothers of all races and all income groups give birth to babies with Down's syndrome. Many of these women will wonder why it has happened to them, and whether there was anything they could have done to prevent their baby being affected. Doctors are fairly sure that Down's syndrome is not linked with anything a woman does, or does not do, during her pregnancy. There is no way of predicting whether someone will have a baby with Down's syndrome.

Mother's age

One factor is linked to the likelihood of having a baby with Down's syndrome – the age of the mother. The older a woman is, the more likely she is to have a baby with Down's syndrome. No one really knows why the mother's age is significant. Although the risk of having a baby with Down's syndrome increases with maternal age, most babies with Down's syndrome are born to women under the age of 35. This is because more women in this age group have babies.

Maternal age statistics

Age of mother	Likelihood of having a baby with Down's syndrome
21	1 in 1600
35	1 in 370
40	1 in 110
45	1 in 35

Right: After having one baby with Down's syndrome, many parents wonder if it will happen the next time they try for a baby.

Will it happen again?

If a couple already has a child with regular Down's syndrome there is a greater chance that their next baby will be affected, too. But it is still much more likely that the next baby will not have Down's syndrome. In a very few cases of Down's syndrome the condition can be inherited – passed down through a family (see page 15).

Genetic counselling

Genetic counsellors are healthcare professionals who help couples who might have an increased chance of having a baby with a genetic condition such as Down's syndrome. They look at the family's health history and arrange blood tests to see whether there are any signs of the inherited form of Down's syndrome. The counsellor will then explain the results and help the couple assess the risks, and explain what choices they have. It is the couple's decision whether to try for a baby or not.

Living with Down's syndrome

Most people find out that their baby has Down's syndrome after it is born, sometimes in the first hours or days, sometimes later. Having a baby is an emotional time for any couple, but for the new parents of a baby with Down's syndrome it can be a period of confusing feelings.

Parents' expectations

When a couple is expecting a baby they usually have some idea of what their new child might be like. When the baby is born with Down's syndrome it is usually a great shock. Parents may feel they have lost something precious; they may grieve for the baby they were expecting to have. Parents may also wonder 'why me?' They may feel guilty, believing that they have somehow caused the baby to have Down's syndrome.

Early days

Some parents feel overwhelmed by the problems they believe having a baby with Down's syndrome may bring. They may find it hard to cope with any immediate difficulties such as the baby finding it hard to feed, or needing a lot of medical attention after birth. These negative feelings can make the first few days or weeks a sad and difficult time. But most parents soon begin to accept their tiny new baby as part of their family.

Welcoming the baby

It is important for family and friends to welcome the new baby with Down's syndrome; to show that he or she is a valued member of the family right from the start. Grandparents can be especially helpful at this time, perhaps finding out all they can about Down's syndrome so that they can support the parents as they begin their new life of caring for the baby.

Most parents of a new baby with Down's syndrome will have very little idea about the condition, or what it may mean for their child. It is very important for them to find out the real facts about Down's syndrome. There are Down's syndrome support groups in many countries and these publish information leaflets and provide helplines for new parents wishing to find out more.

"At first I felt devastated – how would I cope? But soon I let everyone know I was proud of my bouncing baby boys!"

(Fiona, mother of twin boys in the UK, both with Down's syndrome)

A baby with Down's syndrome can bring as much joy as any other new arrival.

Milestones in development

Children with Down's syndrome are all individuals and each will follow their own pattern of development. It is clear, though, that those with Down's syndrome tend to develop more slowly than others, both physically and mentally. This means that they usually reach their **milestones** – recognizable points in development – later than other children (see table on page 25).

Babies with Down's syndrome tend to be smaller than other babies and have a lower birth-weight. Healthcare staff use special charts to monitor the growth of babies and children with Down's syndrome. Babies with Down's syndrome usually have poor muscle tone – they are said to be 'floppy'. This can make it much harder for them to develop physical skills such as holding up their heads, sitting up and walking.

It is natural for parents to compare their own children to others. It can be hard for a parent of a child with Down's syndrome to see other children develop more quickly, to see their child apparently being 'left behind'. It may be frustrating for parents if their child cannot do the same things as other children of the same age. But each child develops in its own time, and parents soon learn to enjoy all of their child's achievements, whenever they happen.

Young people with Down's syndrome reach puberty – sexual maturity – in their early teens just like others. They, too, will experience the mood swings, the strong emotions and the uncertainty that can go along with the physical changes in their bodies. As with all teenagers, the young person with Down's syndrome may find their relationship with their parents becomes stormy at times. The teenage years can be challenging for everyone in the family!

Physical milestones

Milestone	Child with Down's syndrome	Other children
Holds head steady	3–9 months	1–4 months
Sits alone	6–16 months	5–9 months
Reaches out and grasps object	4–11 months	2–6 months
Passes object from hand to hand	6–12 months	4–8 months
Stands alone	1–3 years	9–16 months
Walks alone	1–4 years	9–17 months
Builds a tower of two cubes	1–3 years	10–19 months
Copies a circle	3–5 years	2–3 years

Living with Down's syndrome

Language and communication

Humans are social animals and so communication is one of the most important skills they need to learn. This can be a challenge for children with Down's syndrome as most have some difficulties in developing speech.

Speaking involves the use of a lot of small muscles in the tongue, face and throat. In people with Down's syndrome these muscles tend to be more 'floppy' and so it is much more difficult for them to form words that other people can understand. Many parents of children with Down's syndrome say that their youngsters sometimes have difficulty in being understood by people outside the family. In many cases a child with Down's syndrome will see a **speech therapist** – a healthcare professional who is trained to help develop correct speech.

It soon becomes obvious to parents of children with Down's syndrome that their children can understand what is being said to them a long time before they can speak themselves. And although those with Down's syndrome, especially children, may speak in simple short sentences, they can usually understand when others speak to them in longer and more complicated sentences.

"Sam sometimes came home from school in tears because a group of children had been teasing him at recess, making fun of the way he spoke."

(Shelli, USA, mother of Sam who is eleven and has Down's syndrome)

Other types of communication

A child with Down's syndrome may be two or three years old before he or she says their first words, but that does not mean that they have not been communicating. All infants learn to express themselves through sounds and gestures before they can use real words, and this is true of children with Down's syndrome, too.

Many parents have found it helpful to use sign language alongside speech to help them communicate with their children with Down's syndrome. Sign language is not used to replace speech, as it might be with those who are deaf, but can be used for a short time while speech is developing. When the child becomes better at understanding and using speech the sign language is no longer needed.

Using sign language as well as speech can really improve communication between a child with Down's syndrome and his or her parents.

Living with Down's syndrome

Education

Children with Down's syndrome used to be sent to special schools for those with learning difficulties. Today more and more of them attend **mainstream schools**, where they join in classes with children of all abilities. This is known as '**inclusion**'.

Most people think that inclusion is much better for children with Down's syndrome as they have the chance to make friends and be part of an ordinary school community. It is also good for the other pupils at the school as they can learn about the challenges of life with a disability from first-hand experience.

In class

Many children and young people with Down's syndrome are taught in ordinary classes of children their own age but have special learning plans designed for their individual needs. This means that some of the time they will be doing the same work as the rest of the class, but not all the time. They may have the help of a learning support assistant.

Handwriting can be a problem for children with Down's syndrome, mainly because their muscles are weaker. For children with Down's syndrome, computers can be a great help, as they find it easier to type or use a mouse than to use a pen. In many schools other children in the class are encouraged to help their friend with Down's syndrome by explaining the lesson, or writing things down for them.

Success for Kerry

Kerry is 18 and she has Down's syndrome. She lives with her family in Australia. Kerry did well at her local school. She remembers, 'When I was 13, I went to high school and I left last year at the end of Year 12 with my School Certificate and Certificate of Achievement.'

Kerry also loves sports and was selected to represent her school and her state in swimming. She won Gold, Silver and Bronze medals, and everyone at school cheered for her.

Not everything was easy though. Kerry says, 'I loved high school and I made a lot of friends, but there were times when I was tormented and laughed at, and that hurt my feelings … Mum taught me not to take any notice and to be proud of myself because she was proud of me.'

This girl has fun helping her classmate, who has Down's syndrome.

Living with Down's syndrome

Teenagers with Down's syndrome

In many ways, teenagers with Down's syndrome are just like all teenagers. They have the same wide range of interests, like the same music, watch the same TV programmes and enjoy the same activities. Like all teenagers, young people with Down's syndrome want to make friends and fit in with others the same age. And many wish their parents would let them have more freedom! In the past, teenagers with Down's syndrome would not really mix with other young people because they did not have the chance to meet them. Now that many go to mainstream schools they are making friends and enjoying everyday teenage activities.

Many teenagers with Down's syndrome see their friends being allowed to start making decisions about the way they live their lives – who they see, where they go and what they do – and they want the same independence. Independence can mean going out to the shops or using public transport alone, handling their own money or even having a romantic relationship. This can be a worrying time for their parents, who want to protect their children but also do not want them to feel left out. With the support of friends, many teenagers with Down's syndrome can take the first steps in becoming independent from their families, something which is very important for later life.

Growing and changing

Young people with Down's syndrome become sexually aware in their early teens just as others do. They notice their bodies changing and start to become interested in boyfriends and girlfriends. Information about sex and growing up is just as important for teenagers with Down's syndrome as it is for others. Many teenagers with Down's syndrome form special friendships with others of the opposite sex, and eventually some marry.

Special activities

In some places there are clubs or groups just for young people with Down's syndrome. Meeting together gives these young people a chance to share their experiences with others, and to join in with fun activities and events to help them build up self confidence. Some young people with Down's syndrome have formed their own groups. These may be just for fun, or to offer support and advice to others. As one member of such a group in New South Wales, Australia, says, 'Who better to give advice about Down's syndrome than people with Down's syndrome?'

Teenagers with Down's syndrome fall in and out of love, just like their friends do.

31

Living with Down's syndrome

Adult life

There are now many adults with Down's syndrome living happy and productive lives within our communities. Like other adults, the concerns of people with Down's syndrome revolve mainly around work, health and family life. Doing a worthwhile job is important for a person's self esteem. It gives people a chance to make friends, be independent, earn money and achieve a position in society. This is true for adults with Down's syndrome just as it is for others. A lot of the work done by people with learning disabilities in the recent past was carried out within schemes that had been designed especially for them. This meant that most of the people they worked with also had a learning disability, and the range of work provided was usually quite narrow. Many people now think it is better for people with Down's syndrome to work in ordinary workplaces, and that employers should be encouraged to offer such work. The large chain supermarkets, for instance, employ many people with Down's syndrome. In some countries the state offers support for individuals with Down's syndrome to help them get, and then also keep, real jobs. Many countries also have anti-**discrimination** laws, which make sure that employers treat all people fairly, no matter what their disability, colour, sex or religion.

This man with Down's syndrome has found enjoyable work at a garden centre.

Having children

Many people with Down's syndrome get married, often to another person with a learning disability. Many women with Down's syndrome are fertile, which means that they can have children. Men with Down's syndrome, on the other hand, are not usually able to father children.

ɛɛI am now employed in a part-time job as a clerk in a bank. I like doing the work and I have made friends there.ɟɟ

(Ruth Cromer, 28, who lives in Sydney, Australia and has Down's syndrome. She also works as an actress.)

Ageing

With improved healthcare, people with Down's syndrome are now living longer. Many babies born with Down's syndrome today can look forward to a life of around 60 years or more. The number of elderly people with Down's syndrome is increasing. One of the health issues for older people with Down's syndrome is **Alzheimer's disease**. This is a severe form of dementia, a condition that leads to memory loss and the gradual loss of the ability to perform simple tasks or communicate effectively. It can happen to any older person, but for some reason Alzheimer's disease starts much younger in people with Down's syndrome.

Society and Down's syndrome

People with Down's syndrome want to be part of everyday society, enjoying all the benefits of a good education, an interesting job and having a wide range of friends and interests. They have every right to all these things, so why is it sometimes hard for them to achieve them?

Other people's attitudes

The main obstacle that people with Down's syndrome face is not their learning disability but other people's attitudes. Many people just do not understand Down's syndrome or what people with Down's syndrome are capable of. Because those with Down's syndrome may look or act slightly differently, other people sometimes treat them badly. But the situation is improving. A lot of work has been done by the various Down's syndrome organizations to educate others, and to make sure that people with this condition are treated equally. As more children with Down's syndrome attend **mainstream schools**, and more adults become employed in the workplace, people with Down's syndrome are becoming more visible and are starting to take their rightful place in society.

Myths about Down's syndrome

Society's attitudes towards people with Down's syndrome are often based on a lack of knowledge about the condition. Common myths include:

- *'People with Down's syndrome are always happy and affectionate.'*

This may seem like a kind thing to say but actually it assumes that all people with Down's syndrome are the same. People with Down's syndrome are all individuals and, like everyone else, they have different characters.

- *'Only older mothers have babies with Down's syndrome.'*

Older mothers do have a higher chance of having a baby with Down's syndrome but most babies with Down's syndrome are born to younger women. This is because there is a higher birth rate in this group.

- *'People with Down's syndrome all look the same.'*

There are some characteristics that are typical of Down's syndrome, but people with Down's syndrome look more like other members of their family than others with the same condition.

- *'People with Down's syndrome do not live very long.'*

Although this was true in the past, today many people with Down's syndrome live for 60 years or more. Some are in their 80s, although this is rare.

"My little brothers are so cool and great fun to play with. Just because they've got Down's they don't have to be treated differently."

(Simon, aged 13, older brother to twins with Down's syndrome)

35

Health issues

Some medical conditions are found more commonly in people with Down's syndrome than in others. These range from minor problems such as coughs and colds, to more serious conditions such as **heart defects** and **leukaemia.** However, with good medical care most people with Down's syndrome can lead full and healthy lives.

Heart defects

Around 40 per cent of all babies born with Down's syndrome have a heart defect of some sort. This can range from a heart murmur to a serious abnormality requiring surgery. When a baby is born with Down's syndrome the doctor carefully examines him or her for signs of a heart defect. It is important that these defects are found as early as possible so that they can be treated. Babies with Down's syndrome will then be checked regularly throughout their first few years to make sure that no heart problems have been missed. The doctor may need to use special tests to check the heart such as chest X-rays, electrocardiograms (electrical tracings of the heart), echocardiograms (ultrasound examinations) and cardiac catheterization (sending a fine wire through the arteries to the heart).

Heart defects can have a serious affect on a baby. Abnormalities of the heart and major blood vessels affect the way blood flows through the heart and lungs. This may put a strain on these organs and often has the effect of stopping the baby from growing and gaining weight properly. In very severe cases the baby may die. Heart surgery is needed to correct the more severe heart defects seen in babies with Down's syndrome. This is usually done in the first few months of life and, in most cases, no more surgery will be needed. Today, with modern surgical techniques, many babies that would previously have died can grow up and live full and active lives.

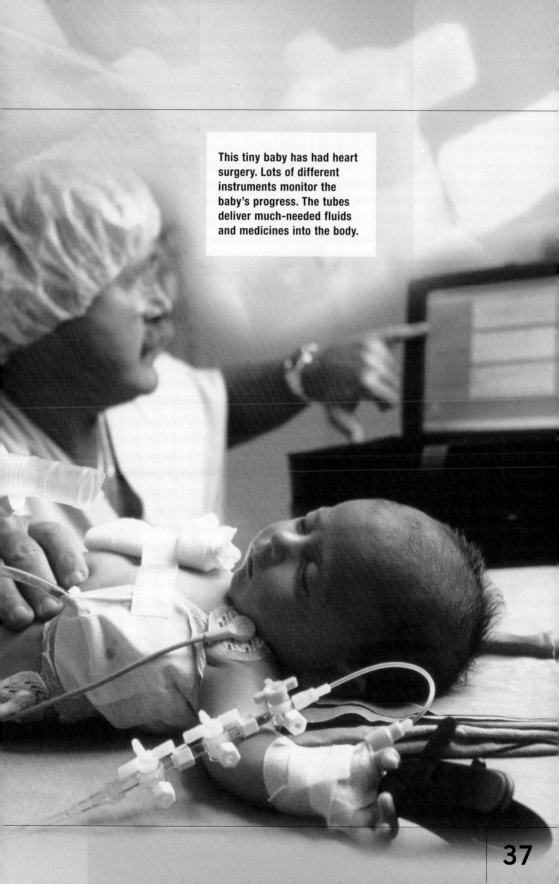

This tiny baby has had heart surgery. Lots of different instruments monitor the baby's progress. The tubes deliver much-needed fluids and medicines into the body.

Health issues

Hearing and vision

Many children and adults with Down's syndrome have some amount of hearing loss, and visual problems are also common. In children these problems need to be picked up and treated as soon as possible before they affect education and development.

Hearing loss

Over half of all people with Down's syndrome have problems with their hearing. These problems may be temporary and treatable, or may be permanent. In children, temporary deafness is usually due to a condition called '**glue ear**', which is fairly common among all children. Glue ear is caused by a build up of sticky fluid in the middle ear, which stops the tiny ear bones vibrating properly. It happens because the tube that normally drains fluid from the ear into the back of the mouth becomes blocked, usually after repeated colds. Permanent deafness (sometimes called nerve deafness) may start in early childhood in those with Down's syndrome but is more common in teenagers.

It is very important that all babies and children with Down's syndrome have regular hearing tests. The earlier a problem with hearing can be picked up, the sooner it can be treated. Many children and adults with Down's syndrome who have hearing loss, including nerve deafness, are helped by wearing **hearing aids**.

A boy with Down's syndrome, who is deaf, chats with his mum in sign language.

Eye problems

Eye problems are common in children and adults with Down's syndrome. People with Down's syndrome tend to have the same conditions that occur in other people, just more frequently. Around one in five children with Down's syndrome have a **squint**, which is when the eyes point in slightly different directions. Because of this the child should have regular eye examinations by an eye specialist. Special glasses usually solve the problem, although occasionally surgery is needed.

Many children with Down's syndrome are found to be either long or short sighted, so it is common to see people with Down's syndrome wearing glasses. About 3 per cent of children with Down's syndrome are affected by **cataracts**, where the lens of the eye becomes cloudy and vision is affected. The cataracts may be present at birth or start later in life, and are sometimes so severe that the whole lens needs to be removed in an operation, with the child needing special glasses to see.

Many people with Down's syndrome need to wear glasses to correct eye problems.

Health issues

Other health issues

Although many people with Down's syndrome remain in good health, there is a wide range of medical conditions that can particularly affect them. As well as heart defects, vision and hearing problems, and a higher chance of developing **Alzheimer's disease**, they also have an increased risk of getting infections or other illnesses. Some of these problems are explained below.

Increased risk of infection

People with Down's syndrome are more likely to get infections – diseases caused by bacteria and viruses. The most common are those affecting the **respiratory tract**, such as coughs and colds.

Thyroid disease

The thyroid is a gland in the neck that produces hormones to regulate the body's **metabolism** and growth. In up to 30 per cent of people with Down's syndrome the thyroid does not produce enough hormones. This can cause serious problems such as slow growth, skin disorders, constipation and poor development of the brain in children. This can be treated quite well with medicine.

Intestinal disturbances

Intestinal disturbances are quite rare, but more common in people with Down's syndrome than those in the general population. One of the most common is **Hirschprung's disease**, where part of the bowel has no nerve supply resulting in severe constipation. An operation is needed to treat this.

Leukaemia

Leukaemia is cancer of the blood cells, a rare but serious disease, which, if not treated, can be fatal. Anyone can get leukaemia but it is more common in people with Down's syndrome (although still very rare). Most cases are in young children under five. There are now some treatments available that greatly increase the chances of survival.

Diabetes

Diabetes is a medical condition where the body does not make enough of the hormone insulin, which controls the level of sugar in the blood. People with Down's syndrome are more likely to get diabetes than others, and may need daily injections of insulin to stay healthy.

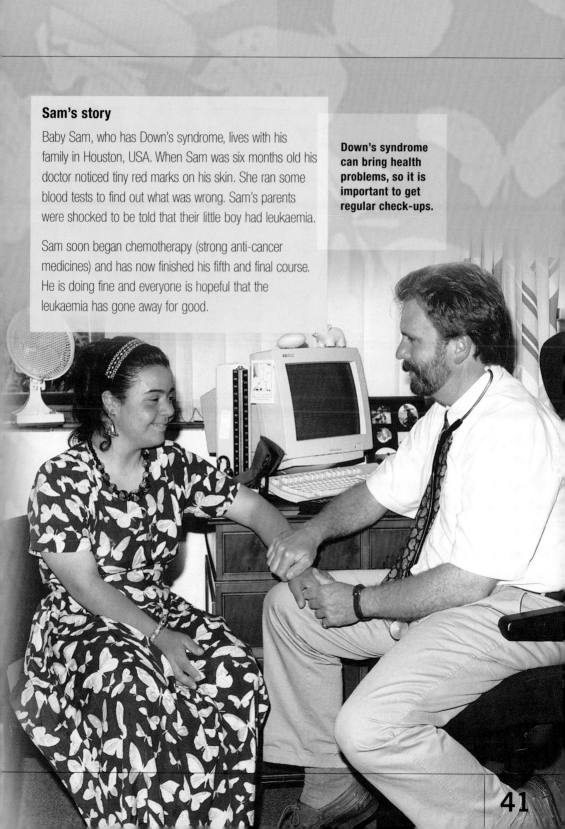

Sam's story

Baby Sam, who has Down's syndrome, lives with his family in Houston, USA. When Sam was six months old his doctor noticed tiny red marks on his skin. She ran some blood tests to find out what was wrong. Sam's parents were shocked to be told that their little boy had leukaemia.

Sam soon began chemotherapy (strong anti-cancer medicines) and has now finished his fifth and final course. He is doing fine and everyone is hopeful that the leukaemia has gone away for good.

Down's syndrome can bring health problems, so it is important to get regular check-ups.

Treatment

Prenatal testing means having tests done before a baby is born to see whether he or she has a particular condition, such as Down's syndrome. This allows the parents and healthcare professionals to plan for the care of the baby before it arrives. It may also allow the parents to make a choice about whether they wish to continue with the pregnancy, or to end it with a termination (also called an abortion). There are two groups of tests: screening tests, which give an indication of how likely it is that the baby has Down's syndrome, and diagnostic tests, which can say for certain whether the baby is affected.

Screening tests

Most pregnant women are offered at least one screening test between the 15th and 18th week of pregnancy. These tests do not harm the baby. The mother's blood may be tested for the amount of certain substances it contains, produced by the developing baby. Together with information about the mother's age, weight and length of pregnancy the blood tests give an indication of the likelihood of the baby having Down's syndrome. Ultrasound tests use sound waves to get a picture of the unborn baby. They provide information about whether the baby is developing normally. In some places a special early scan is offered, which can give an indication of whether Down's syndrome is present or not.

Diagnostic tests

Because they carry a small risk of causing a **miscarriage**, diagnostic tests are used only when there is a high chance of the baby being affected (such as in women over 35 years old). The only way of diagnosing Down's syndrome is to find the extra **chromosome** in the baby's cells.

Chorionic villus sampling is a test that can be done around the tenth week of pregnancy. A thin needle is inserted through the vagina and cervix, or through the abdomen, to take a sample of the developing **placenta** (the organ that attaches the baby to the mother's womb to allow transfer of food and oxygen), which has similar cells to the baby. About 2 per cent of tests end in a miscarriage.

During amniocentesis a needle collects fluid from around the baby. The doctor uses ultrasound pictures to guide the needle to the right spot.

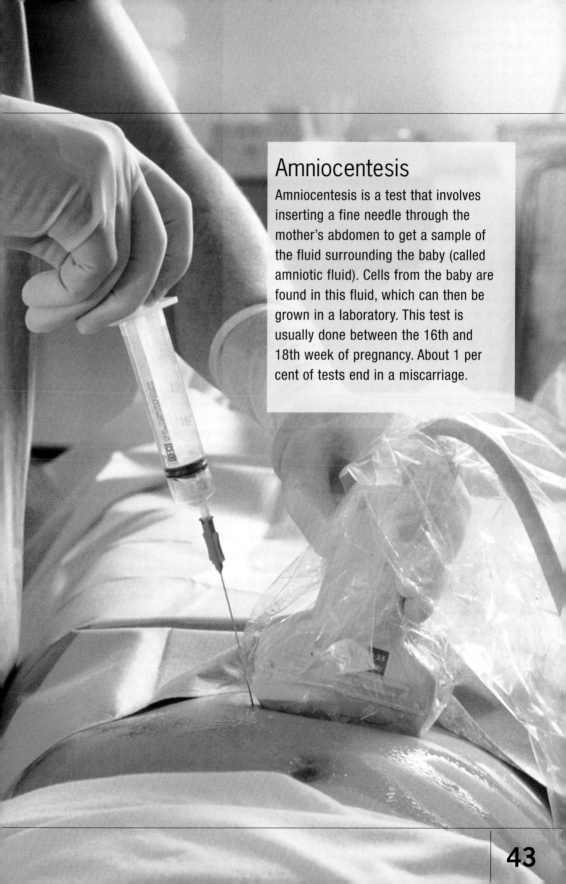

Amniocentesis

Amniocentesis is a test that involves inserting a fine needle through the mother's abdomen to get a sample of the fluid surrounding the baby (called amniotic fluid). Cells from the baby are found in this fluid, which can then be grown in a laboratory. This test is usually done between the 16th and 18th week of pregnancy. About 1 per cent of tests end in a miscarriage.

What can be done?

Down's syndrome is not a disease. There is no medicine or other treatment that can be given to make it go away, it is something a person lives with for the whole of their life. But there is a lot that can be done to help people with Down's syndrome live healthier, happier lives and achieve as much as possible. And the best way to start is through a process called **early intervention**.

Early intervention

Early intervention is a programme of activities, exercise and physical therapy specifically designed for the first years of life of a baby with Down's syndrome. The first three years of life is a very special time. It is when the brain is most eager and able to learn new things. In the past people did not expect much from infants with Down's syndrome and so many missed out on the kind of attention that others were given at this stage.

Now it is clear that early intervention really helps a baby's development. In many developed countries, it is offered to all babies with Down's syndrome. Starting soon after birth, parents are offered help and encouragement with various aspects of their baby's development. This might mean the help of a **physiotherapist (physical therapist)** to devise special exercises for the baby, the help of a **speech therapist** to encourage the use of language, or advice being given on using play to help the baby develop.

But with all this special help it is also important that children with Down's syndrome should meet and play with other children. For this reason most parents are encouraged to enrol their child into an ordinary playgroup so that they can be with others of the same age.

Unproven treatments

Over the years there have been many claims about treatments that help those with Down's syndrome. These include special diets, vitamin supplements, medicines and injections. It can be really tempting for parents when a new treatment comes forward that claims to help. A lot of research has been carried out to try to find out if any of these treatments have any effect on Down's syndrome, but there is currently no evidence that they do.

Physical activity and play are important for young children with Down's syndrome.

Support

There are many different ways in which people with Down's syndrome and their families can be supported.

Friends and family

Many parents feel sad and confused when they first have a baby with Down's syndrome. Friends and family can make all the difference by showing that the new baby is someone to be loved and accepted. If the new baby is picked up, cuddled and admired just like any other baby it will reassure the parents at a difficult time.

Being part of a loving family and community helps all children to grow and fulfil their potential. As a child with Down's syndrome gets older and moves into adulthood, support from their friends can help them to leave the care of their family and become independent.

Professional help

Doctors or midwives who break the news to the parents that their baby has Down's syndrome can be very supportive by having a positive attitude and giving clear information about the condition. As the child grows up, he or she may need the support of healthcare staff to help with the various medical conditions and illnesses that can be associated with Down's syndrome (see pages 36–41).

With support from volunteers, children with Down's syndrome can enjoy exciting activities like horse-riding.

This fun-runner is raising money to help people with Down's syndrome.

In many developed countries the government provides help, including financial benefits, to families with a child with Down's syndrome. There may be support for education and, later, help with finding a job or specially designed work placement. Many people still feel that not enough is yet being done in supporting people with Down's syndrome in our communities, but things are improving.

Down's syndrome organizations

Over the years, parents of children with Down's syndrome, healthcare staff and others with an interest in Down's syndrome have set up organizations to offer support and information to new parents and others. These organizations include the National Down Syndrome Society in the USA and the Down's Syndrome Associations in the UK and Australia (see pages 52–53). They provide information leaflets and telephone helplines as well as campaigning for the rights of people with Down's syndrome.

"It is the goal of the National Down Syndrome Society to ensure that all people with Down syndrome are provided the opportunity to achieve their full potential in all aspects of community life."

(The National Down Syndrome Society, USA)

Can modern science help?

The future for people with Down's syndrome is likely to be most affected by improvements in the way they are treated by society, rather than by scientific advances. However, there are a number of ways in which modern science may be able to help.

Genetic research

Down's syndrome is caused by the presence of an extra piece of genetic material – an extra **chromosome** 21. A lot of research is being done to try to find out exactly how the extra copies of these genes affect the growth and development of a person with Down's syndrome. Finding out which genes are on chromosome 21 has been made easier by the Human Genome Project, in which scientists have mapped out all the genes that are present on human chromosomes. It is unlikely that genetic research will ever lead to a cure for Down's syndrome, but one day it may be possible to block the extra genes so that they have less effect.

Modern medicine

Many babies with Down's syndrome used to die in their first years of life due to the medical complications that can occur, especially **heart defects**. Advances in modern medical science have meant that most babies now survive and live longer, healthier lives. And the research continues. For example, one of the studies being done at the moment looks at **Alzheimer's disease** in people with Down's syndrome, and another looks at whether giving certain vitamins or minerals helps the development of children with Down's syndrome.

Better prenatal testing

A lot of research is being done to find safer, more accurate ways to discover whether an unborn baby has Down's syndrome. Modern science may one day find a quick and safe test for Down's syndrome that could be made available to all pregnant women.

However, many people who support those with Down's syndrome feel that this would be a bad thing. If more women are tested, more may choose to end the pregnancy and so fewer babies with Down's syndrome would be born. Most parents and carers of people with Down's syndrome feel that it is wrong to end a pregnancy just because the baby has this condition.

This laboratory technician is screening amniocentesis samples, using a special machine. But does technology like this help people with Down's syndrome?

Looking to the future

The future has never looked brighter for people with Down's syndrome. Where once they were kept in institutions or in the home, separate from other people, today they are beginning to take up their rightful place within society. Babies who were once thought of as having no future are now thriving within their families and growing into healthy, happy children. And, little by little, adults with Down's syndrome are becoming more visible in their communities as they find worthwhile jobs and learn to speak up for themselves.

Increasing public awareness and understanding is leading to increasing acceptance of people with Down's syndrome within our schools, workplaces and communities. As more individuals with Down's syndrome enter our society, more people have the chance to meet them and make friends. This is the best way to break down barriers between people and get rid of the fears and suspicion that often surround disability.

Today, expectations are much higher for people with Down's syndrome.

High expectations

Today's adults with Down's syndrome were brought up at a time when most people thought that there was no real point in stimulating and educating children with Down's syndrome because they would never be able to learn very much.

The adults of the future with Down's syndrome will be different. Parents now know that they can have much higher expectations of their children with Down's syndrome. **Early intervention** programmes and **mainstream schooling** are helping children with Down's syndrome to achieve more than many people ever thought they could. Who knows what they might achieve in the future?

Changing attitudes

Much of the change in attitude towards people with Down's syndrome has been brought about by the hard work and commitment of their parents, together with others such as healthcare workers who care greatly for those with this condition. The organizations they have formed have worked tirelessly to raise awareness of Down's syndrome and to make sure that people with Down's syndrome are treated well and fairly.

It is now up to the rest of society to accept individuals with Down's syndrome and make them feel welcome in their own communities.

Information and advice

Many organizations have been set up around the world to provide information about Down's syndrome and to support those who are affected by it. Many have websites that can be easily accessed by anyone who wants to know more.

Contacts in the UK

The Down's Syndrome Association
155 Mitcham Rd, London, SW17 9PG
Tel: 020 8682 4001
Website: www.dsa-uk.com
Email: info@downs-syndrome.org.uk
The Down's Syndrome Association exists to support people with Down's syndrome, their families and carers, as well as providing information for healthcare professionals. The website has many useful links to other sites.

The Down Syndrome Educational Trust
Website: www.down-syndrome.info
Email: enquiries@downsed.org
The Down Syndrome Educational Trust provides an information network offering a range of information resources and online services to the international Down syndrome community.

Down's Syndrome Scotland
158/160 Balgreen Rd, Edinburgh, EH11 3AU
Tel: 0131 313 4225
Website: www.dsscotland.org.uk
Email: info@dsscotland.org.uk
Formerly the Scottish Down's Syndrome Association, this organization works to improve the quality of life for everyone with Down's syndrome in Scotland.

Mencap
123 Golden Lane, London EC1Y 0RT
Tel: 020 7454 0454
Website: www.mencap.org.uk
Email: information@mencap.org.uk
Mencap is the UK's leading learning disability charity working with people with a learning disability and their families and carers.

Contacts in the USA

The National Down Syndrome Society
666 Broadway, New York, NY 10012
Tel: 212.460.9330 (9.00 a.m. to 5.00 p.m. Eastern time)
Toll Free: 800.221.4602 NDSS
Website: www.ndss.org
Email: info@ndss.org
This organization was set up to increase public awareness of Down's syndrome, offer support to parents and encourage research. A section of their website, 'Club NDSS', is especially designed to be used by people with Down's syndrome.

Contacts in Australia

The Down Syndrome Association of South Australia
Office address: 24 Harrow Avenue, Magill SA 5072
Mailing address: c/o Tranmere North Post Office, Tranmere SA 5073
Tel: (08) 6363 3510
Website: www.downssa.asn.au
This organization offers support and a wide range of services to people with Down's syndrome and their families throughout South Australia.

The Down Syndrome Association of Western Australia
4/1136 Albany Highway
Bentley WA 6102
Tel: (08) 9358 3544
Free phone: 1800 623544
Website: www.dsawa.asn.au
This organization provides support for new parents of a baby with Down's syndrome, offers information and runs events for those with Down's syndrome.

Down Syndrome Association of Victoria
495 High Street, Northcote 3070
Tel: (03) 9486 2377
This association provides parents, families and friends of children and adults with Down's Syndrome with support, encouragement, information and resources.

Contacts in New Zealand

New Zealand Down Syndrome Association
PO Box 4142, Auckland, Ph 0800 NZDSA I
Tel: 0800 693724
Website: www.nzdsa.org.nz
Email: national.coordinator@nzdsa.org.nz
The NZDSA promotes the interests of people with Down's syndrome and their families by providing information and support through regional groups and networks.

Further reading

Books and pamphlets:
Living with Down's Syndrome, by Jenny Bryan; Hodder Wayland, 2000

People with Down's Syndrome – Your Questions Answered, by Susanna Seyman; Down's Syndrome Association, UK, 2002
Answers to some of the questions most often asked about Down's syndrome.

Your Baby Has Down's Syndrome, by Sarah Rutter; Down's Syndrome Association, UK, 2000
A 23-page booklet for new parents (and other relatives). Also available from the Down's Syndrome Association in Arabic, Bengali, Chinese, Gujerati, Punjabi, Spanish, Urdu and Welsh

Fiction:
The Falcon's Wing, by Dawna L. Buchanan; Orchard Books, 1992
After her mother's death, 12-year-old Bryn moves with her father to a rural community in Canada to live with her elderly aunt and her cousin, Winnie, who has Down's syndrome.

Red Sky in the Morning, by Elizabeth Baird; Heinemann, 1998
A teenager comes to terms with the notion of disability when her brother is born with severe disabilities. This book is suitable for older children and teenagers.

Disclaimer
All the Internet addresses (URLs) given in this book were valid at the time of going to press. However, due to the dynamic nature of the Internet, some addresses may have changed, or sites may have changed or ceased to exist since publication. While the author and Publisher regret any inconvenience this may cause readers, no responsibility for any such changes can be accepted by either the author or the Publisher.

Glossary

Alzheimer's disease
a disease of the brain that causes loss of memory and inability to think clearly. This condition is more commonly found in elderly people, over the age of 65.

cataracts
a condition where the lens of the eye becomes cloudy instead of being completely transparent (see-through). It causes problems with vision.

chromosomes
tiny structures within each cell of the body. They carry the genes that hold inherited information, which can be passed on from a parent to a child.

conceived
a baby is conceived when the egg from the mother and the sperm from the father meet and start to form new life. This is also known as the time of conception

diabetes
a condition in which the body is unable to process sugar and starch properly, resulting in high levels of sugar in the blood

discrimination
unfair treatment, usually based upon a person's colour, sex or medical health

early intervention
in the case of babies with Down's syndrome, this is a programme of activities, exercise and physical therapy specifically designed for the first years of life

epicanthic fold
a fold of skin which runs vertically between the upper and lower eyelid at the inner corner. Anyone can have this condition, but it is more common in people with Down's syndrome.

foetus
the medical name given to an unborn baby that is still developing in its mother's womb

genetic counsellors
professionals who give expert information and advice to couples about their chances of having a baby affected by a genetic condition

glue ear
a medical condition affecting the inside of the ear, which becomes filled up with thick, sticky liquid. It causes temporary hearing loss.

hearing aids
small devices that help a person with hearing loss hear better by making sounds seem louder

heart defect
an abnormality of the structure of the heart, present from birth

Hirschprung's disease
a medical condition affecting the intestine where there is an area of bowel that cannot contract because it has no nerve cells

hypotonia
the medical word for 'floppiness' due to the muscles being too relaxed

inclusion
the process by which someone with a
disability is included into mainstream schools
and everyday society rather than being kept
separate in special institutions

intestinal disturbances
upsets and illnesses of the intestines (or gut),
where food is digested

leukaemia
a rare type of cancer, or malignant disease,
which affects a person's blood cells

life expectancy
the number of years for which a person is
expected to live

mainstream schools
schools that the majority of children attend,
rather than special schools, where the lessons
are designed particularly for children with a
disability

metabolism
the rate at which a person's body breaks
down food and turns it into energy

milestones
important stages that mark the development
of a child, such as learning to crawl, taking
the first steps and saying the first words

miscarriage
the natural loss of an unborn baby during the
early stages of a pregnancy

Mongolism
the old, and now unacceptable, name for
Down's syndrome

mosaicism
a rare type of Down's syndrome where only
some of the cells of the body have the extra
chromosome 21

physiotherapist (physical therapist)
a healthcare professional who helps with
special exercises to develop and maintain
normal muscle actions

placenta
the organ that attaches the unborn baby to
the mother's womb to allow transfer of food
and oxygen

respiratory tract
those parts of the body involved in taking
oxygen from the air; the nose, windpipe,
airways and lungs

speech therapist
a healthcare professional who helps a person
develop correct speech

squint
an abnormal condition affecting the eyes,
where one points in a different direction
to the other

translocation
the process by which a piece of one
chromosome moves across to become
attached to another

trisomy
the presence of a third copy of a chromosome
in a cell, where there should only be two

Index

Titles in the *Need to Know* series include:

Hardback   0 431 18840 8

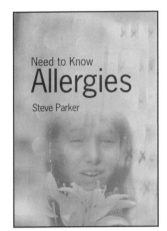

Hardback   0 431 09760 7

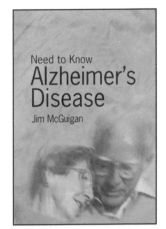

Hardback   0 431 18841 6

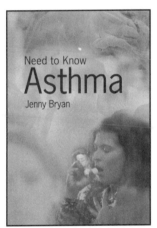

Hardback   0 431 09761 5

Hardback   0 431 18842 4

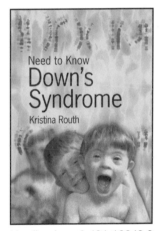

Hardback   0 431 18843 2

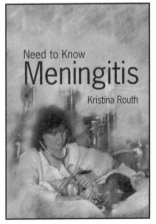

Hardback   0 431 18844 0

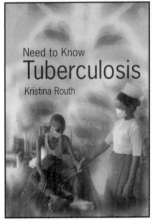

Hardback   0 431 18845 9

Find out about the other titles in this series on our website www.heinemann.co.uk/library